D1557664

White Silk,
Dark Chocolate,
and a Little Bit of Magic

Life is good and we are good in it.

Barbara Herrick

Conari Press

First published in 2010 by

Red Wheel/Weiser, LLC

With offices at:

500 Third Street, Suite 230

San Francisco, CA 94107

www.redwheelweiser.com

ISBN: 978-1-57324-481-7

Library of Congress Cataloging-in-Publication
Data is available upon request.

Cover and text design by Tracy Johnson.

Typeset in Alita, Aphrodite, Fairplex, Odile, and
Today Sans.

Cover and text illustration © 2009 by friztin.

Printed in Hong Kong

GW

10 9 8 7 6 5 4 3 2 1

We enter our Glory Years full tilt,

our heads and hearts high.

Our midyears are when we finally find

OUR PLACE AND OUR PEACE,

when we are powerful,

when we are well and well-rewarded,

when we're the best at what we do,

when we discover that

life is good,

and we are good in it.

Our minds are deep and clear,

our hearts are

fierce and **full,**

our souls unafraid.

Whether we are alone,

IN TANDEM OR IN FAMILY,

whether we are

scientists,

artists,

nurturers,

or activists,

or all of those things at once,

whether we have achieved all of our dreams

or are just beginning to find them,

whether life has been fair or whether it has not,

we know

our **strength**, our **spirit**, our **will**,

and our **direction**.

we trust our bodies.

Striding in long lengths across our chosen paths, we walk.

WE SWIM IN DEEP WATERS.

WE DELIGHT in a

stunning red dress and *sexy three-inch heels,*

but we won't wear them long—

we have places to go that require

a wilderness of spirit

AND SHOES TO MATCH.

Knowing pain and loss,

ache and misspent hope,

we have survived our own lives

and found a pathway

that sustains us.

Pleasure

is ours for the taking:

the feel of warm sand on bare feet,

what a gin and tonic can do for a hot August afternoon,

the feel of *silk* on bare skin,

what a good man's hand can do for a Sunday morning.

WE TRUST OUR MINDS.

Gathering in quilting groups and reading groups,

we talk over creamy coffee or blackberry tea

or a purple wine,

DARK AND MYSTERIOUS AS THE WAYS OF THE WORLD.

And talk.

And talk.

And talk.

taking in ideas,

THROWING THEM OUT,

working them over

until we understand in our bones.

Gossip loses its salacious edge.

It's not that we don't talk about people,

we do.

But our gossip arises from our care for people

and what happens to them.

When we bump into an old friend on a walk,

and she tells us of her recent divorce and surgery,

a question we are most likely to ask is this:

What are you reading that helps you through this?

We are transported by

painting and sculpture,

by dance and poetry,

by music.

We are drawn to the arts as

dreamers and creators,

because we are

SURE OF WHAT WE HAVE TO SAY.

we are drawn to the sciences

because we are

hungry for the why of the **why** of things.

We are drawn to politics and business

because we can no longer be turned away from those

endeavors and because

those institutions desperately need us.

Always we **teach.**

Always we **nurture.**

Always we **mentor.**

We trust our hearts.

No longer disdainful of our own tears,

we cry easily and often,

in pleasure and in pain.

we laugh over our own lunacies

and indulge other people

as they sort out their own.

We are intense in our loyalties

and our passions;

our friendships are sustained over decades;

as is our work,

our art.

A child can rend our heart, as can an honest man.

We have an ever-growing capacity for joy.

Life, more often than not, seems

mysterious, fragile, intensely beautiful,

terrible in its consequences,

blessed in its graces.

We are spiritual.

Either sustaining our traditions with a quiet absoluteness,

or finding another that serves us better.

—

Some of us may have thrown off the traces and

walked barefoot around the world.

We believe in angels, either the sublime beings,

or in the more unsentimental angels:

each other.

We pray.

We trust great intuitive leaps,

the power of love,

a sensibility of gratitude,

and a profound acceptance

of **life** as it is.

OUR KINDNESS IS AS A STATE OF GRACE.

We are not amused

by drugs or the abuse of alcohol.

We are not amused by the lack of funding for education

or the lack of protection for unwed mothers.

We are not amused by hungry children in our own city.

We are not amused by people who neglect or

abuse their own bodies or any other.

Nor are we amused by an overt and degrading sexuality

foisted on the most vulnerable of our daughters.

We are wearied by war,

knowing that it implodes,

as well as explodes,

destroying its makers as well as its victims.

We know what needs to be done.

We will do it.

We trust our unhappiness.

Whether in relationships that confine us or

jobs that demean us,

we find that depression or anxiety are based on

real factors in our lives.

We reject the notion that something is wrong with us,

and embrace the knowing

that something is wrong.

We will attend to it, rather than continue to bleed

emotionally, physically, spiritually, financially.

We love our men.

They have literally given us life,

and we honor our HUSBANDS and our FATHERS for that.

Our BROTHERS have sharpened our sense of humor,

made us giggle at unlikely times,

shared a sense of adventure, **been our best friends,**

our most enduring conspirators.

We may have married young

or waited a while.

We might have tossed out the men who were

marginal, confining, mean, or untrustworthy.

We might have found

a true gem

who needed no polishing,

or we might have found

a sturdy fixer-upper

and done our best with him.

We might have had one true love, or

learned to love in sequence

or in total.

At some critical point we learned to love

our old guys in a whole new way.

We can sustain friendships with men

that are not sexual,

AND WE CAN LEER WITH THE BEST OF THEM.

WE LOVE OUR SEXUALITY,

as it comes these days

from a deep biology,

from our most interior selves.

Sex is no longer skin-deep

and in our Glory Years,

WE ARE INTERESTING LOVERS.

We are *beautiful*.

BEAUTY IS NO LONGER ONE-DIMENSIONAL

or unachievable.

We are beautiful no matter what shape our bodies.

The lines in our faces soften our countenances.

Our silvering hair forms halos around our faces.

We exude

light and *energy,*

INTELLECT and WILL,

passion and folly,

pleasure and pain,

strength

and a little bit of magic.

We have reinstalled the *stars* in our eyes.

WE ARE MOTHERS,

nourishing and **nurturing**

the children who were born to us

and the ones who were not,

the ones within our families,

and the ones within the larger family

that inhabits our Earth.

We trace our heartbeat

back to our mother's heartbeat,

to her mother's heartbeat,

and to the mother before that

until we reach clear back and sense

our first mother's heartbeat

and the breath of Mama God.

That original energy is ours,

the gift and heritage of spirit and biology.

Our power is broad and deep,

and the world is changing

because of our touch, our words, our breath, our pulse.

We know that the control over our own lives

extends no further than our fingertips,

but that our influence is *infinite*.

We choose our forevers carefully.

Dedicated to

Julie Herrick

COUSIN AND CO-CONSPIRATOR

Breast Cancer Warrior

The Essence of Hope

For my family, here and away,

for my rich circle of friends,

for my Alive! family at the Cathedral of the Rockies,

and for Jan Johnson and the crew at Conari,

all of them kind and brilliant both, a heart-felt thank you.